Ch  Beg ...ers

How to Awaken and Balance
Your Chakras

Heal Yourself with Chakra
Healing, Reiki Healing and
Guided Meditation

Table of Contents

Introduction

Alternative and holistic forms of healing and wellness are becoming increasingly popular today, especially among those who have inadequate or even a complete lack of balance in their lives and want to achieve said balance enough to keep healthy and focused each day. One way that a person's energy is determined is by chakras, which is anything but a new concept, despite modern society being more embracing of these alternative forms of healing and wellness.

When one thinks of the word "chakra", colors will most likely *immediately* come into mind. A psychic can determine one's current mood or energy by color. For example, if a psychic sees a blue aura around a person, then that person has the blue chakra around them - they, at that moment, are in a calm, relaxed state. Or, if the psychic sees a red aura around another person, then that person is fully committed, grounded or focused on a task, career, etcetera.

However, when one is in pain, ill, or low on energy, these chakras will not work to their full potential or, in many cases, not at all. Hence, many would trust crystals and gemstones as forms of healing, and not just for the physical body. For example, to strengthen the red chakra, one may place a crystal or gemstone on the spine, that way you can regain your sense of focus and drive towards your tasks and goals.

The book further explains the chakras in detail, as well as the specific gemstones and crystals to use to reawaken the appropriate chakras.

Chapter 1

The Chakral Basics

Those who are not necessarily spiritually inclined—and even those who *are*—do not always realize that their moods, amounts of energy, and motivation are connected to their chakras. A person who feels unmotivated, unsocial, and rather sluggish one morning at work can attribute this to a misalignment and/or weakness of chakra. It may even be the feeling of being surrounded by the negative energies of the managers and other coworkers. Again, one does not have to be super-spiritual in order to acknowledge, understand, and learn about chakras.

The concept of chakras was first discovered by Hindus in the 7th century BCE. They discovered the different energy points of the human body and that the soul can be found in different parts of it.

They included these concepts in their sacred writ called the *Upanishads.* The Goddess Shri Lalita, who is said to reside in Mount Meru, is the deity often depicted in the pictures that'd you'd see of a woman's form colored in chakra points. She also represents the junction of both masculine and feminine energies in addition to the concept of all powers from different parts of the body working together.

Keeping Chakral Alignment

If one chakra is out of whack, then *all* the chakras are misaligned and negatively affected since they must all work together to keep the energy flowing throughout the body. You must learn to keep them all under control even if one chakra is more affected than another.

Once you know how to keep all your chakras under control and keep them unblocked, then energy flows freely. Hence, you will feel more motivated, driven and even more pleasantly social towards others. It is not difficult to learn to control your chakras, but it does take some hard work and commitment to *keep* the good energy flowing inside of you. Not only is this important in keeping yourself focused on everyday life and tasks, but also in keeping yourself in good health. Poor health and focus *never* go hand-in-hand. Once you get the hang of keeping your chakras aligned, you'll notice your life becoming much easier.

Too much energy in one chakra can be just as bad as insufficient energies in another. For instance, if you open your red chakra too much, you may end up wearing yourself rather thin if you take on more tasks at a time than you should. You, then, most likely would not have enough energy and focus to complete all of these tasks properly and successfully—or at all. If it's open enough to work properly, then you have enough sense to take on only as many tasks as your current energy allows so that they can be done properly and on time. Also, other workers can have a chance to take on these tasks and get them done properly and in a timely fashion as well.

Homes of the Soul

The Brahma Upanishads talk about four main places in the body where the soul stays: head (the state beyond the physical human experience), heart (dreamless sleep), throat (dreaming), and navel (waking life). On the other hand, the Yogattava Upanishads believe that the body parts are linked to the main elements of earth, fire, air, and water.

When one says they see an aura around someone, referring to a color, the color represents a person's current energy and vibration state. For instance, if you are currently experiencing constant sadness throughout the day, which is obviously natural and understandable, sometimes that energy can be transferred to another person and cause them to also feel low and sad, which in turn can hinder *their* daily activities as well.

However, if you're in a room filled with cheerful people that positive energy can transmit into *you*, leaving *you* in a happy, cheerful mood, in turn priming you to transmit said energy to others as well.

Wheels and the Sun

Wheels and the sun are two symbolisms associated with chakras. Wheels represent a constant flow, be it as part of an automobile or a water wheel. Meanwhile, the sun symbolizes order and balance, which are the main sources to keep our energies flowing, as the sun gives us energy as well. In fact, the word chakra means "wheel of light".

Chakras can sometimes become completely damaged, but this does not have to mean a permanent state, so long as you understand and acknowledge that they are in your body.

Again, all energies, negative and positive, will have an overall effect on your health. If a person is in a constant state of anger or sadness, they will be more susceptible to falling into poor health not only physically but also emotionally, and in some cases even mentally.

Misaligned or imbalanced chakras are equal to *chemical* imbalances, all of which can cause sudden mood swings. All you need to do is learn how your chakra points work and you will soon be on your way to a more stable emotional state.

The Body's Chakras and their States

Your body has a total of nine chakras: seven main ones and an additional two that don't come around very often. You shouldn't focus as much on the two additional ones though, because the seven main ones are usually the most affected by your moods and energy levels.

A chakra is always in one of these three states: open, blocked or sealed. When a chakra is open, it radiates the most energy and absorbs the most healing and alleviation from pain, illness, or other negative feeling or state. However, the *only* way to receive any form of healing from alternative practices is if the chakra is fully open.

A sealed chakra is not to be confused with a blocked chakra. In fact, a sealed chakra is actually a form of protection from negativities entering inside of you.

Finally, a blocked chakra is an unhealthy chakra, as you are most susceptible to absorbing negative energies and a lack of flow of *positive* energies.

The seven main chakras will now be explained in further detail.

The Earth Star Chakra

The Earth Star chakra connects you to the Earth's elemental energies, keeping you more rational, logical, and focused instead of acting or speaking before thinking. These color auras are black, maroon and silver, and the best gemstones to use with this chakra point, often beneath your feet, are hematite, garnet, tiger's eye, and onyx.

Onyx and hematite are considered the go-to gemstones for blocking out negative energies. Earth star chakras just goes to show that the more grounded you are in your everyday life and conscious decision-making, the more enjoyable life becomes. Conversely, when this chakra is blocked, you are more susceptible to depression, lack of interest in connecting with others and loss of motivation to do *anything*.

The Root Chakra

The root chakra, represented by the color red, is responsible for your family and survival aspects, in addition to how well you work and/or socialize within groups. Its point is at the tailbone of the spine and is believed to be the "root" of all chakras, hence its name.

In terms of physical health, when the root chakra is opened, your skeletal and circulatory systems are more likely to be healed, as well as your legs, feet, hips, and parts of the excretory system. The proper stones to use should be in the red and black family, such as obsidian, bloodstone, ruby, garnet, red jasper and red quartz. Keep this chakra balanced and you will see that you will work better with others and use rational-thinking to help out groups of people when need be, especially when problems arise.

The Sacral Chakra

This chakral point is found in the lower abdominal area. It is in charge of a person's sense of desire for adventure and connection with other people, as well as sense of pleasure, wealth (not necessarily in terms of finances) and sexuality, especially when it comes to understanding your partner's needs and desires.

Other concepts relevant to the sacral chakra are creativity and fiscal responsibility. Its color aura is orange, and the gemstones associated with keeping the sacral open are coral, carnelian, and amber. With these gems, you will feel motivated to finish your projects, especially creative ones, properly and in a timely (but not rushed) manner. You will also have the ability to better understand someone's feelings, as well as your own.

When the sacral chakra is blocked, you will be more susceptible to moodiness and lack of sexual desire or pleasure.

The Solar Plexus Chakra

The solar plexus chakra (also called navel chakra) is found in the upper abdominal area and when open, allows you to be in control of your own life, with confidence and no fears, while keeping your self-esteem high. Your confidence and self-respect, however, will not be limited to yourself—you will have faith in others too, albeit in a rational, reasonable sense.

The color aura is yellow, and the right stones to use, especially when you have illnesses and digestive discomfort are gold topaz, citrine, amber, gold calcite or any other stone in the yellow/gold family.

Any negative energies associated with this chakra are lack of self-worth and no sense of real self.

The Heart Chakra

The heart chakra deals with love, and not just in a romantic sense but also an overall *compassionate* one. It allows you to be loving and in a state of joy and peace, which in turn will allow you the ability and desire to heal others when they are sad and/or in some form of pain, be it physical or emotional. It also allows you to be charitable to the less fortunate.

The heart chakra's colors are green and pink and the appropriate stones to use would be: rose quartz, moss agate, emerald, jade, and aventurine.

Keep this chakra open in order to keep your respiratory system healthy and functioning properly. Also, remember that love and compassion, even the smallest gestures, will go a long way.

The Thymus Chakra

The thymus chakra is similar to the heart chakra, as far as unconditional love and compassion are concerned, only that there are more concepts involved. The thymus, located between your throat and your heart, is more in charge of allowing you to be accepting of others no matter what and without judgment. The thymus is also in charge of the endocrine system, which deals with growth, but not solely in a physical sense.

The colors associated with the thymus are green, purple and aqua. The appropriate and best stones to use are lapis lazuli, aquamarine, and turquoise.

When this chakra is blocked, you lose your ability to understand and accept others. Moreover, it becomes harder for you to show real love towards people and to accept any advice they would have to help you grow, particularly in a spiritual sense. You would also lack the ability to have lucid dreams or even good dreams for that matter.

The Throat Chakra

When the throat chakra is opened, you are able to better communicate and express your emotions to others, especially in a clearer, more confident manner while still being respectful. You also have an increased sense of creativity and can make rational decisions.

Located in the throat, it is responsible for bringing out all of your *soul's true feelings*. Hence, you'd be capable of hearing and communicating with spirits. Its color is a light blue hue. The gemstones you'll need to keep this chakra healthy are: sodalite, aquamarine, lapis lazuli, and turquoise.

When this chakra is blocked, any body part related to the mouth and throat will be negatively affected, as well as your overall intellectualism and curiosity.

The Third Eye Chakra

Located at the forehead, the third eye chakra helps you to "think outside the box", think for yourself, and at the same time, hinder shortsightedness or narrow-mindedness when it comes to others' viewpoints and inputs. Although this chakra allows you some form of psychic ability and communication with spirits (even the ability of astral projection), keep in mind that there is still a power higher than yourself.

You will find the third eye chakra in the center of your forehead. Think of the colors violet or a very dark blue with this chakra. With that being said, the gemstones amethyst, lapis lazuli, and fluorite are most effective here.

The nervous system is associated with this chakra, so in order to keep the third eye open, make sure you are mentally stable and that all five of your senses are working properly. When this chakra is weakened, you quickly lose interest in things and activities that once excited you, and you criticize others – and yourself—far too much. You would also experience major creative locks.

The Crown Chakra

This chakra connects you with the spiritual world and enhances your awareness of it even more than you imagined in addition to aiding you to enlightenment. It enables you to live in the moment with no worries or regrets because your mind is in a clear state. However, when this chakra is blocked, you will be unable to let go of past hardships and issues and are more likely to influence you to become depressed and narrow-minded.

The chakra point here is at the very top of your head, and its colors are white, purple and gold. If your brain and spine hurt, use selenite and clear quartz for healing.

Keep in mind that this is the most important chakra of all, so be sure to take extra care, as it can affect your other chakras, both negatively and positively.

The Soul Star Chakra

The soul star chakra represents the light that is found in all the other chakras. It also allows you to connect with spirits and be in tune with your soul to completely understand it, as well as the good things that the universe and life have in store for you. Located just above your head, the best gemstones for this chakra are Lemurian seeds and selenite. Meanwhile, the aura color is white.

Chapter 2

Consciousness and How Chakras Evolve

Chakras are often referred to as the centers of consciousness. Often, what comes out of your mouth will dictate where your emotions and how your days and life will go. This state will tie in with your ability and capacity to think before speaking and acting.

It is said that the best ways to activate your chakra are yoga and meditation. Both practices can bring you to a higher state of consciousness and keep the mind clear, focused, and grounded.

Evolving Chakras

Often, you will see pictures of color auras forming in a vertical line from a figure's spine to the top of its head. That line shows where the seven main chakra points are located. All your thoughts and emotions are inside its appropriate points. Your consciousness and focus are the two main factors that deal with the kind of energy you currently have and how it flows or doesn't flow.

When you lose focus and your thoughts become unclear and disorganized, your flow is weakened. However, it is still up to *you* and *only* you to determine how this energy flows, because it is up to *you* to decide how you will deal with the negativities of others and your surroundings. Being physically ill and/or in pain or discomfort also takes a severe toll on your overall energy, even sometimes causing you to lose it altogether, albeit for a short period of time.

The stronger your energy flow, the more aware you are and the more spiritually inclined and connected you will be.

The following paragraphs will explain the seven levels of consciousness, tying in with each main chakra point.

The First Tier of Consciousness: Root Chakra

Humans, so far, have the most sophisticated levels and understanding of consciousness. However, keep in mind that despite your level of spiritually inclination or connection, you are still a human being dependent on the basic necessities such as food, shelter, water, and adequate rest for survival.

Past feelings, memories, and lessons learned from past events are stored inside the root chakra. While it is still okay to feel sadness or pain, the root chakra becomes stronger if you learn lessons from past mistakes and learn to deal with past tragedies or other painful memories in a constructive manner.

Allowing these past hardships to define your life will hinder your improvement in the present and the future, so much so that it can cause long-term health problems down the road.

To keep this chakra balanced, chant a mantra to yourself. For example, reassure yourself that you are strong and protected. Meditation is also important. Try to imagine yourself connected, or rooted and firmly grounded, to the Earth, hence the name "root" chakra.

Do *not* rely exclusively on gemstones for this chakra, or any of the other chakras. It's important to get your healthy nutrients in, too. For this chakra, carrots, beets, potatoes and any other vegetable that grows out of the ground are your best bet. Also, be sure to pay attention to proteins, such as eggs and legumes. If you can handle spicy foods, hot peppers are also highly beneficial.

The Second Tier of Consciousness: Sacral Chakra

Here is where you develop your own sense of self, in part with the choices you in what and with whom you surround yourself. You develop communication skills and learn to enhance them properly. With this development of your own identity, you are not only shaping yourself but also how you interact and connect with other humans, and the kinds of romantic, familial and friendly relationships you build with them.

To balance the sacral, reassure yourself that you are creative and that you love and are passionate about life. When you meditate, rest your hand on the lower abdomen and picture an orange light and imagine it surrounding you, freeing you from worry and self-critical feelings. The more conscious the sacral, the more dedicated you are to your realistic goals, without anything to stop you from achieving them, albeit by positive, non-hurtful means. The right food would be oranges, strawberries, melons, vanilla, honey, and cinnamon.

The Third Tier of Consciousness: The Solar Plexus Chakra

In this state, you already have your own identity shaped will now develop your very own way of articulation, although some of it may be influenced by the methods of speaking from others, especially from those that live in close proximity to you. It also allows you to learn from and correct your own mistakes so they don't carry over to the rest of your life. In its strongest form, you have full control and grasp of your own life, without having to rely on *anyone else* to help shape it for you. You have the complete freedom and street-smarts to live your life and plan your future on YOUR own terms.

To prevent this chakra from blockage, use such mantras as "I control my own destiny" and picture a yellow/gold aura around you.

During meditation, fix your eyes on the flame of a fireplace or a candle and imagine a flame igniting inside you, giving you your own strength. Your grains and dairies are most essential for awakening and strengthening the navel chakra.

The Fourth Tier of Consciousness: The Heart Chakra

This stage allows you to fully see the true joy and beauty in life, particularly in the simplest and smallest things. It also allows you to give love and compassion fully and experience both in return. Negative feelings are removed from your mind and body when this stage is at its peak, and you also focus much less on materialistic things and more on the deep meanings of life.

For mantras, reassure yourself that you love all the world and that you, in return, are loved. Your meditation sessions should consist of focusing on someone you love and assuring yourself that you will be happy and healthy, and in return wish everyone you love the same sentiments. Also learn to look past not only your own mistakes and flaws but the mistakes and flaws of others, too.

Foods that are essential for heart health are mostly the green vegetables, especially those with leaves and herbs.

The Fifth Tier of Consciousness: The Throat Chakra

In its strongest stage, your communication skills and ability to vocally express your emotions openly and without worries are at their peak. It also shows that you have already established the full ability and confidence to think for yourself and not be swayed by the opinions of others. However, keep in mind that it is never okay to express yourself in a mean-spirited, bullying, and abusive way.

To keep this chakra healthy, drink herbal teas such as lemongrass and fruit juices particularly in the citrus family. During meditation, assure yourself by repeating mantras related to living life only on your own terms.

The Sixth Tier of Consciousness: The Third Eye Chakra

This stage allows you to experience senses beyond the basic five of smell, taste, touch, hearing, and sight. You will also have full understanding of what it means to be truly connected to the universe. However, take care that you do not let your ego get in the way, overinflate, or become grandiose. These kinds of actions can lead to headaches and inability to understand others and their feelings. Moreover, you may become very judgmental rather than a supportive listener.

At meditation, picture a ball of indigo blue around you. The best foods to keep this chakra working properly are found in the blue/purple families, such as eggplant, blueberries, and anything containing sage, rosemary, and lavender. Also, keep a supply of walnuts handy.

The Seventh Tier of Consciousness: The Crown Chakra

Here, you are at your highest consciousness level, where you develop wisdom from past mistakes and even past accolades. However, keep in mind that life itself is a learning process and experience. To grow from this experience is to remember that we are all one and connected to the whole universe.

At the seventh tier, you also become deeply connected in the spiritual sense, and the higher power is by your side. Actually becoming one with the higher power, however, is a near-impossible feat, as it is very rare that one reaches this level of consciousness and mindfulness, but you are still completely aware and mindful when you do reach this stage.

No mantras are needed here, just silence to ensure your mind is at its clearest. Close your eyes and imagine a white light fully radiating inside of you.

Drink plenty of water and avoid any and all processed foods to keep this chakra open and working to its fullest potential. Once you are able to reach this stage, you are completely at peace and quietude.

Chapter 3

Chakras and their Benefits

As mentioned earlier, when one chakra is not working properly, it is most likely that all the other chakras will become misaligned and malfunction as well. Hence, you can't just focus entirely on one chakra and forget about all others. Remember that each chakra has its own unique purposes and benefits.

The Root Chakra

The root chakra is responsible for enabling you to keep a firm grip on reality and to be focused on and work toward *realistic* goals. It also allows you to properly manage your finances and remain practical with them; and maintain an abundant

36

supply of healthy survival resources, such as food, water, and shelter. Thus, you can enjoy living a healthy life and have the motivation to always keep moving forward. This chakra also aids in the flow of energy towards the rest of your chakras.

The Sacral Chakra

If you are having trouble socializing and connecting with people and enjoying activities you normally love, that means your sacral is unbalanced, leaving you feeling unpleasant. Once you manage to get the sacral opened and balanced, you can enjoy and appreciate life and the company of others much more.

The Solar Plexus Chakra

When you feel confident enough to live life completely on your own terms with no regrets or shame afterward, then you know that enough positive energy is flowing throughout the solar plexus or navel to make it work. You acknowledge that you are worthwhile and serve a good and positive purpose in this world. Thus, you maintain a good company for yourself and everyone else around you.

The Throat Chakra

Your ability to effectively communicate and express your feelings and thoughts in a non-hurtful way but also without timidity depends on how well the throat chakra works. You also need to learn to keep a happy medium with communication, which means speaking up enough to fully express your thoughts to others, while at the same time giving the others the chance to express *their* thoughts and not judge and belittle them for having thoughts different from yours.

The Third Eye Chakra

An inability and/or unwillingness to see through the perspectives of others and an overall closed-minded, short-sighted mentality will result in an unbalanced, weakened third eye chakra point. It also deters you from being creatively inspired and/or motivated, and you will also become disconnected from the spiritual world.

The Crown Chakra

This is the highest point in your body (literally at the top of your head) and its strong form allows you to experience a full connection with the spiritual realm with the acknowledgment of your inner beauty and state of complete bliss. You are completely confident in living your life to its richest and fullest. Moreover, you become one with yourself and the spiritual world.

The reason it's crucial to keep *all* of your chakras aligned at once and at all times is so that you remain fully healthy and focused. For example, if your throat chakra is opened too wide but your root chakra isn't opened enough, or at all, then you can end up carelessly speaking of whatever comes to mind—in this case, not in a good way—while aiming for lofty, unrealistic life goals for yourself and boasting about them, resulting in others not taking you as seriously as you would want them too.

Although it may seem rather difficult at first, it *is* possible to find ways to keep your chakras all aligned, be it through methods such as meditation, exercise, or maintaining healthy, balanced eating habits.

Chapter 4

Awaken Your Seven Chakras

It takes work to keep all your chakra points opened and aligned especially since they are not going to activate automatically. There are exercises, both physical and breathing, used for each chakra in order to "wake" them up, so to speak.

Root Chakra

Stand in a comfortable position with your feet hip-width apart. Rotate your hips from right-to-left 50 times, while breathing deeply.

Repeat the step above, only this time you'll move your hips from left-to-right.

Solar Plexus / Navel Chakra

Suck your stomach in as far as you can while breathing deeply 50 times. However, don't suck in your stomach *too* far. It is important that you experience no pain while performing this exercise.

Heart Chakra

Stretch your arms from side-to-side and in a circular motion, while breathing deeply 49 times. Then, move your arms in an up-and-down motion, while taking 3 breaths.

Throat Chakra

Bend your head down so that you're facing the ground and roll it to the left, to the back and now forward. With each head roll, breathe deeply 7 times.

Third Eye Chakra

Raise your eyebrows and take 49 deep breaths. Then close your eyes and focus on the breathing.

Crown Chakra

Lift up your arms above your head and take 7 breaths.

All humans absorb energy from others, both positive and negative. If you absorb negative energy, then you, in turn, will become bitterly angry, or even ill. These feelings may be the results of unbalanced chakras, but it is solely up to *you* to get your feelings under control.

To restore balance to your chakra points, create for yourself a private space free of noise and distractions. Surround yourself with natural elements or your gemstones and crystals. You should also imagine color and light auras surrounding you.

To connect with your spirit guide, say phrases of assurance and prayers. Remind yourself that you are free to express your true feelings and love and feel loved as your soul truly feels and desires. You are also completely free to live life the way you want, with no one stopping you.

Test your chakra points by waving your hand around each point to make sure each one is working.

Chapter 5

How Chakras Help with Your Endocrine and Immune Systems

Endocrine System

The Endocrine system keeps the hormones responsible for your movement and growth under control. Your hormones go right through your bloodstream in order to maintain both mental and physical health. Below are the glands associated with the endocrine system.

Pituitary

The pituitary is the main gland that ensures your other glands are working properly. Found connected to the hypothalamus between your eyes, it is responsible proper movement and maintaining an all-around healthy body.

Pineal Gland

Melatonin, a hormone that aids in a regular sleep pattern, is produced by your pineal gland. The pineal and pituitary gland must work together in order to keep your third eye chakra at its strongest and to also enable and maintain proper physical movement.

Pancreas

Not only does the pancreas help you digest food properly and produces enough insulin for breaking down sugars, it also keeps your energy levels under control.

Ovaries

Found only in females, they are responsible for releasing eggs for reproduction.

Testes

Found only in males, they release testosterone and sperm for the purpose of procreation and reproduction with females.

Thyroid

The thyroid, if healthy, keeps your heart beating at a normal pace; your metabolism under control; your bones and muscles healthy and strong; and also aids in keeping the brain healthy. Thyroxin, produced by the thyroid, is also responsible for converting the food stored in our bodies into energy.

Parathyroid

The parathyroid controls calcium levels in order to keep the nervous system and muscles working properly, as well as keeping the bones healthy.

Hypothalamus

The hypothalamus is responsible for our reactions to external temperatures, hunger, thirst, and pressure while sending all of these kinds of messages to the brain and other major organs.

Adrenal Glands

The adrenal glands send messages to organs regarding reactions to chemicals and pain.

The Immune System

When your cells are improperly functioning and not fully restored, you become weak and ill. Although medicines may work to resolve a weak immune system, you must make sure that you take care of your chakra points as well.

Thymus Gland

The thymus plays a major part in keeping the immune system healthy.

Chakra and Glands

The locations of each gland are placed at, or near, all the different chakra points.

Root Chakra

Connected to the adrenal glands, the root chakra is responsible for maintaining physical energy and a healthy immune system and metabolism. It also helps you fight off nervousness, fear, worry, and insecurity.

Sacral Chakra

Aids in sexuality to keep both male and female reproductive organs and glands functioning well. Both you and your partner will fully experience pleasure and joy during sexual relations when the sacral is open and strong.

Solar Plexus Chakra

The pancreas controls the energy levels in your body. When the solar plexus chakra is open, your metabolism remains normal and steady, as do your digestive system and memory.

Heart Chakra

The heart chakra controls the thymus gland in order to maintain a healthy heart, both physically and emotionally, as well as the ability to love. Keep your heart and nervous system healthy and balanced by lightly tapping the area between your chest and collarbone a few times, especially when you feel yourself becoming tense and high-strung.

Throat Chakra

The throat chakra keeps the thyroid gland under control and helps prevent fevers and chills of the body. It also helps to maintain a healthy immune system, in all these forms: physically, emotionally and mentally.

Third Eye Chakra

The third eye chakra is responsible for keeping the main (pituitary) gland functioning properly so that all the organs and other glands can function properly as well. If the third eye chakra is weakened or unopened, the pituitary gland, as well as the other glands, will have problems functioning. Consequently, every one of your body systems will be negatively affected.

The pituitary gland, while working with your pineal gland, helps maintain and gain intelligence and conquer learning curves. Above all, however, to keep both these glands working together *well* and efficiently, you must keep a clear head and

52

soul while avoiding undue anxiety on any negative obstacle that comes your way.

Crown Chakra

The crown chakra ensures our sleep patterns are regulated and maintained while also helping maintain an all-around well-being.

Again, when one chakra negatively affects a gland, it is more than likely all the other chakras will be affected, in turn causing problems to all the chakras' respective associated glands.

Chapter 6

Chakras and the Solar System

Many people do not think that chakras would have any astronomical connections in any way, shape or form, especially with the solar system because astrology is not particularly touched-upon in modern society, even though older practices such as crystal healing and holistic/alternative medicines have been adopted and well-utilized. Each of the seven main chakras is connected with some the planets, and here is how:

Crown Chakra

Associated with Uranus, your crown chakra enables you to see your surroundings as through the eyes of whichever Higher Power you choose or believe in. However, the only way to truly open this chakra would be to lose all your senses of ego and pride. Moreover, you must take care of any unfinished earthly business you have before fully committing yourself to this chakra, no matter how long it takes you.

Third Eye Chakra

Associated with Neptune, the third eye chakra helps you manage time and acknowledge how limited it might be for you on this earth. You are, thereby, fully aware and cognizant of the Universe around you. You are open-minded, giving and always willing to expand your horizons, perpetually curious and learning for as long as you are living on Earth. Keep the crown open and you will notice your intuitive sense growing while you also become more willing to listen to the advice of others, both human and spiritual forms.

Throat Chakra

The throat chakra is ruled by two planets, namely: Mercury and Jupiter. This chakra helps you with your effective communication skills and creativity. At its strongest, your speaking skills are most intelligible and you are at your best in effectively conveying your messages and feelings to others with complete confidence. It also helps you be fully confident in just being yourself, without being easily swayed in other directions by others.

Heart Chakra

Venus is the closest associated with the heart chakra allows you to fully experience compassion, peace, and love, on both giving and receiving ends.

Solar Plexus Chakra

Sun and Mars are both in charge of the navel chakra and also help to bring optimism and light to you, especially during your darkest moments. Like the throat chakra, this allows you to shape, without fear and shame, your own complete identity with *no* hindrances or negative influences from others. Shaping your own identity means finding your *own* religious or spiritual path in accordance with your *own* happiness, so long as you're not harming anyone or anything else along the way.

Sacral Chakra

Ruled by Pluto, this brings out the best in you as far as sensuality and tenderness go. When the sacral is open and strong, you show great desire to be creative and sensual. However, if this chakra is open too wide, your only interests and desires at that moment are sexual/sensual. With that being said, you still must be sure that your partner feels up to feeding these desires you have, and that you can meet his or her needs in return.

Root Chakra

Look to Saturn to be your celestial guide in order to keep yourself stable, grounded and focused on all of your goals and a realism to achieve them in a timely yet successful manner. The root chakra, when open and healthy, will send you signals when you are working too hard yet truly achieving very little from it—or nothing at all. The objective is not to remain stagnant in life, but to move forward. If you are unhappy with your current life situation, e.g. your present job, you can always move on to another one that satisfies you, and not merely in a financial sense.

Chapter 7

Problems Chakras Face

If you are struggling with anything such as financial issues, relationship strains, illness, injuries, job-related stress, family problems, traumatic events or other woes, it is natural and normal for you to react with emotions such as anxiety anger and sadness, but you should know at this point that your chakras will become unbalanced and not work properly, and in the worst cases, not at all. Each chakra is related to and affected by different types of negative situations:

Root Chakra

When you feel as though you have worked very hard (physically), but have not achieved enough in order to survive. These sorts of feelings cause joint pains and pains throughout the rest of the body. You will also become ill. If you can't ever get the root chakra balanced, these pains and illnesses can quickly become long-term and in some cases, incurable.

In order to heal the root chakra, you must believe that you are useful in this Earth and serve a purpose in it, keeping the connection in and to this world.

Solar Plexus Chakra

To keep a healthy navel chakra, your self-esteem needs to be higher, especially when you encounter harsh and negative criticism and comments from others. Long-term effects of said low self-esteem include digestive and liver issues. All you need to do to combat and control this negativity is to accept yourself for who you are, while still trying to make any and all self-improvements necessary.

Sacral Chakra

An inability or to express your feelings weakens the sacral, and long-term effects including sexual and reproductive problems, such as lack of any libido, and back and stomach pains. To regain this chakra's health, stay creative, positive and keep yourself occupied with and immersed in activities you love.

Heart Chakra

There *is* such a thing as loving someone (or something) too much, and that actually weakens the heart. You can love someone so much that you could become possessive of them, so much so that you get jealous when that person wants space and some time away from you. These sorts of feelings can cause heart problems and other limb pains, such as in the arm/wrist area. The concept and emotion of love are supposed to be used for positive, uplifting purposes, and *never* for harmful thoughts or intentions.

Third Eye Chakra

When you become too consumed by your emotions, especially negative ones, the third eye chakra weakens. You also become disconnected from this chakra when you have so much imagination inside of you that you forget and are disconnected from events in the real world, thereby delaying your growth, especially in a spiritual and psychological sense.

Keep an open mind to other people's advice, even though you may disagree with them. In the long run, these pieces of advice can actually be beneficial to you, especially in your goal to not just survive but to also serve a purpose in the real world.

Throat Chakra

You need to be able to speak or otherwise convey your messages and thoughts clearly and effectively in order to keep the throat chakra healthy. You must also be able to form your own ideas and sense of *self*. If you are afraid to say what's truly on your mind out of fear of ridicule from others, then you just bottle up. Bottling up, especially for a prolonged period of time, will lead to physical illnesses, mostly related to the ears, nose, and throat.

Crown Chakra

As the highest level of consciousness is found at this chakra point, it is often hard to let go of ego and to accept that there is someone of a higher being than you. In other words, it is really *impossible* to try and complete all tasks yourself with an unrealistic timeframe in which to accomplish them. Of course, you don't want to be lazy or under-achieve, but at the same time, you still must keep in mind that you are human and that it is also impossible to complete tasks or live life with an unclear head.

Chapter 8

How to Heal Broken Chakras

It is not difficult to learn how to repair your own chakras, be it through holistic medicine, crystals or whatever method works best for you.

Root Chakra

Fear, worry, and uncertainty weaken this chakra the most—and the quickest. In order to regain courage and the drive to accomplish your goals to move further in life, here are some things you can do:

1) Give someone a hug, or ask someone to give *you* a hug.

2) Give yourself a back rub for about 15 minutes.

3) Raise a plant at home to keep you more connected with earth and nature, two very important methods of survival and success. Another way to keep in touch with nature is to go for a walk, barefooted.

4) Plan an outdoor picnic.

Sacral Chakra

Feelings of guilt are not good for a healthy sacral chakra. Here's what you can do to help fight that off:

1) Go get yourself a massage to loosen any stiffness and tightness you have in your body. This physical improvement will also help you improve emotionally.

2) Use aromatherapy or Epsom salts when you take a bath. These products help get rid of negative energies.

3) Do something with art to keep your creativity flowing.

4) Get into baking, as it is actually relaxing and therapeutic for both your mind and hands.

5) Write love notes and poetry.

6) Get rid of dirt and all the unwanted clutter in your home. Those are a distraction and deter you from accomplishing what you have planned for the day.

7) Show love and positivity not only to yourself but also to others.

Solar Plexus Chakra

If you find yourself reacting to any kind of traumatic, troubling event--especially when the event is unexpected—in a mature, calm manner, especially when you react overemotionally, then you know that your navel chakra is weakened.

Here are some solutions to help you learn from these events and move on:

1) If someone is directly mean or nasty towards you, fold your hands over your solar plexus to block the negative energy from them.

2) It is natural and perfectly fine to outwardly express your anger, but is *never* okay to take it out on others in harmful ways, physically or verbally. Instead, do something more constructive by writing, drawing or punching a soft object, such as a pillow.

Heart Chakra

If you ever feel unable to love, or that you love someone so much you become bitter and jealous, you need to repair your heart chakra, using some of these guidelines:

1) Think of some of the positive qualities in a person that you admire, but also remember to focus on the positive attributes of *yourself* instead of being self-deprecative. At the same time, don't let your self-admiration devolve into egotism and conceit. You must also be aware of your flaws and how to fix them.

2) Surround yourself with people who respect and encourage your positive spiritual growth. These people don't necessarily have to share the exact same spiritual beliefs as you, but they should be able to help you and help you grow, especially during times of need.

3) Do some yoga and stretching.

4) Get in touch with nature as much as possible.

5) Count your blessings and remember all the good things that happened in your life.

6) Write a list of wishes for yourself, and hopefully, they are realistic enough to be fulfilled one day.

Throat Chakra

Keep your throat chakra healthy and functioning by being honest with others and yourself. Also, keep your creativity awake and get inspired if you feel yourself suffering any kind of creative block:

1) Plan what good things you will do for others each day, even if it's a simple compliment or gesture of kindness.

2) Go an entire day without complaints and take criticism with a grain of salt, no matter how harsh.

3) Sing a song. It's a good release of and from tension.

4) Let external surroundings, such as noises from nature, guide you and aid in your creativity.

5) Listen to any and all good advice others have for you.

6) When someone says something mean or horrible to you, *completely* ignore them.

Third Eye Chakra

Again, the only way to keep your third eye chakra healthy is to be sure to not let your imaginations deter you from having a grip on reality. Here are ways in which you can do that:

1) Look at beautiful artwork and/or watch a beautiful, uplifting film.

2) Plant yourself a meditation garden, with whatever vegetables, fruits and other plants you love most.

3) Decorate your home with uplifting, positive quotes or pictures.

Crown Chakra

No matter how spiritually inclined of a person you are, you must never forget that you're still human like everyone else. In order to acknowledge that so that you maintain your willingness and desire to keep growing as a person, as a delusion of perfection, in addition to a sheltered existence, means no real growth and learning.

1) Reflect on events, both good and bad, of your past and don't let them define you but rather use them as lessons to improve and enrich your life, and to be grateful for all the good things that happen in your life.

2) Keep your spiritual connection and relationship with whatever Deity it is you choose to worship.

3) Be charitable, but not for the praise. Do it because it's TRULY from your heart.

Chapter 9

Crystal Healing for Specific Chakras

Crystals, when used properly, will also aid in strengthening your chakras, in addition to the guidelines given in the previous chapter. However, in order for them to work properly to their full potential, you have to place them directly at your chakra points. Here are the appropriate stones to use for each chakra and why:

Root Chakra

Use garnet, as the root chakra's color is red. It helps you keep connected with nature and the earth, and to lose the sense of materialism, particularly when it comes to things you don't really need or have any real use for. For example, do you really *need* that extra high-profile car in your garage, and eventually all it really does is sit in your garage, collecting dust and dirt? Remember that "keeping up with the Joneses" will *not* get you through life the way it's truly meant to be lived rather than just robotically going through the motions.

Sacral Chakra

Carnelian is the ideal stone for the sacral chakra in order to keep you in tune with human nature and connection to the world. Your creativity and ability to keep your emotions balanced are important as well. With this, you will always feel as if you have a purpose in this world.

Solar Plexus Chakra

Citrine helps keep the negative energies outside of you and away from you. This is another stone that helps aid in and maintains emotional balance in order to focus on not only accomplishing your goals but also doing so in an effective, meaningful way.

Heart Chakra

To keep your heart chakra healthy and balanced, your best bet is the green aventurine to maintain human connection and compassion, as well as to aid in controlling any angry or hostile feelings you may have. It also provides a humbling inside of you, enabling you to realize that *everyone* on this earth needs and is deserving of compassion and love.

Throat Chakra

Jolite helps you best with effective self-expression and open, honest communication. It also helps you determine what works and doesn't work for you, be it physically, spiritually and emotionally. For example, if someone offers you ice cream and you know you cannot have it because of dairy allergies, you can politely refuse and explain why you cannot have it, and when you're polite about it and truthfully explain why you had to refuse it, the less likely that person's feelings will be hurt. Also keep in mind that the best forms of creativity, be it through poetry, song or visual arts, always come from the creator's most *honest* thoughts and life experiences.

Third Eye Chakra

Think of the amethyst as a rather multi-purpose gemstone, but specifically for the maintenance of healthy third eye chakra, it helps you bring peace into your life and helps you deal with stressful events in a calmer, more constructive manner in order to keep in touch not just with the real, carnal world but also your spiritual self. It also helps you not to act or speak without thinking of the consequences or hurt it may cause to others.

Crown Chakra

The rainbow moonstone is as multi-purposeful as the chakra itself. As an actual rainbow contains many colors, the crown chakra is also responsible for aiding in other chakras, if opened and used properly.

This gemstone helps you keep connected and grounded in your own spirituality, and *not* to use it to inflate your ego and act and think as if you're "above" everyone else in this world because of it. Remember, there are different paths of life for different people.

These stones will be most effective and healing if you are in a completely quiet space free of distraction, especially from negative influences. You can hold the crystals above you and rotate them a few times. You will know that these stones are working if you feel any sort of odd sensations.

Chapter 10

Benefits of Journaling to Help Your Throat Chakra

This chapter focuses on your throat chakra and other ways to help you keep honest, open and constructive communication with others and to be honest with yourself at all times.

Many people are often too shy and afraid to expose their true selves for fear of being alone in this world, or just out of fear of ridicule and harsh criticism/judgment. But the thing is this: Not *one* person in this world will be liked by literally *everyone* they come in contact with.

Keeping a journal is an excellent alternative to speaking upfront straight away. Set aside some time each day to write out all your private, innermost thoughts. The more you practice communicating your feelings out, the method of journaling will more likely turn into a springboard for being honest and upfront with people face-to-face rather than a mere substitution for direct communication.

Journaling isn't everyone's thing, though. If this method doesn't work for you, have someone start the conversation for you. The topics can range from something as simple as if you enjoy watching football to something deeper as in how you feel about healthcare reform. If you end up being the only one in the room of people who actually dislikes watching football, so what? All that matters is that you were truthful in your opinion, and you didn't give a "yes" answer just to fit in with the crowd. This is a much touchier subject, but you will not necessarily be ridiculed for being the only healthcare reform supporter in the room, but you will be more respected for expressing your *own* honest opinion about it. People will eventually catch on to you and find you're being a fake if you give a fake opinion, and that is how you lose respect—and friendships—from others.

Chapter 11

How to Love Yourself and Others to Open Your Heart Chakra

If you lack the ability to love, which in turn will not enable you to receive it, then how will you survive on this earth, especially if you cannot love yourself? Thriving in this world without friendship or other meaningful relationships that will help and encourage your growth and success in life is impossible, and not just financially speaking. Practicing love is not difficult if you can change a negative mindset into a positive one, starting with taking the time to understand someone else's feelings.

Real love is never fickle. A fickle love is a kind that attaches you to someone or something for so long.

Eventually, though, you end up suddenly disliking the object of your love when an associate or friend has an opposing thought about them.

There is a saying that goes "you can't truly love anyone unless you love yourself." While it is good to be charitable and kind to others, you must also take time to repair and take care of yourself. If you have the means to take care of someone else yet leave none for yourself, then you will lose the ability to survive and then become bitter because of it, and that progresses to your love for people turning into the opposite: bitterness and hatred. Those people, in turn, will turn bitter and sometimes hateful towards *you in* order to defend their well-being and survival.

Another test of genuine love is if and how you will be by that person's side, despite their flaws or the rough patches they experience. For example, if a mother finds out her child has been arrested for a petty crime, such as shoplifting, it is natural for a mother to be very angry with her child, as she did not raise him to steal, but theft is not a reason for her to disown him. She, as the mother, must be able to give guidelines so that he will never shoplift again, and help him down the right path of life to become a successful and worthwhile adult.

Say a close friend or family member becomes ill to the point they must be hospitalized. It's paramount that you have enough free time, and more, to visit them and help them as much as possible until they are nursed back to health enough to return to their normal lives. What's more, you should still keep the bond going, through happy and rough times.

One of the worst things you can do is sever ties with a person if they suddenly become strapped of funds due to a disaster or other crisis. Again, friendships and relationships are *not* only about happy times and night outs. Severing ties betrays an exploitive spirit, and anyone who uses people for selfish gain automatically loses any and all respect from others.

Another way to show you truly love someone is by forgiving them of their wrongdoings towards you. Forgiveness does take some time, though. However, if this person commits gross wrong, such as murder another loved one or a beloved pet simply out of a fit of rage, then forgiveness can be difficult and near-impossible for you to have. There is always a reasonable balance and medium.

As another saying goes, self-care isn't selfish.

Chapter 12

Yoga and Chakras

Many people turn to yoga in order to maintain not only a good physical balance but also for good mental focus. It also aids in getting chakras to unlock and work to their fullest potential. There are different poses, exercises and stretches to help awaken different chakras.

For the root chakra, the best poses and exercises are the warrior pose, lunges, squats and chair pose, while focusing on your pelvic area.

Deep and forward lunges, along with hip exercises and the chair pose work in order to awaken your sacral chakra and pleasurable sensuality and to have desires beyond unnecessary material ones.

Do yoga twists in order to keep the navel chakra healthy and active so that you can fulfill your ambitions and never lose passion with them.

If you're unable to do backbends, it is best you learn to do them eventually to keep a balanced heart chakra so that you learn to combat feelings of disappointment and loneliness. Your ability to love unconditionally and to be truly compassionate will show and even improve with the help of this exercise.

For a balanced throat chakra, do the fish pose, the plow, the camel and the shoulder stand. Not only will these exercises aid you in keeping in touch with the spiritual world, but also effectively keep in touch with those in the real, mortal world.

The healthy third eye chakra keeps you well in touch with the real world as well as making sure you realize that you're not a robotic existence—you do have a purpose in this world that you must find, unlock and utilize. The best exercises are the chair poses and simple breathing exercises.

For the crown chakra, you can implement pretty much any pose or exercise, but whichever you choose, keep in mind that they will only work if you first let go of your ego and make sure your other chakra points are healthy and in check as well.

Chapter 13

Using Meditation to Help Your Chakras

Meditation works particularly best when done first thing in the morning, in order to have a clear, focused mind for the entire day. In order to have a successful meditation session, though, you need to be in a quiet, private space completely free of distractions and allow yourself to just relax for a few moments. For mediation, you do not have to work on *all* your chakras at once. In fact, it is best to focus on one that you're struggling with most at that particular moment.

Start by sitting perfectly upright, back straight, sitting Indian style, but be sure you're comfortable. Then close your eyes and focus on the sound and pattern of your breathing. There are specific ways of meditation for each chakra.

For the root chakra, focus your energy on the color red, and think of a red light aura around you. This takes as much time as you personally need.

For the sacral chakra, focus on your inner child and the color orange.

Now, you can move onto the navel chakra and focus on the color yellow and positive ways to deal with criticism from others.

Think of the color green when focusing on the heart chakra and also focus on love, compassion and how you will receive and also transmit those feelings to others in a proper way.

Blue is the color you should have pictured in your mind when your meditation session centers most around the throat chakra. You should also focus on being your own person and how you will use your sense of true self when dealing with the day ahead of you.

Indigo is your spirit color when you move your focus onto the third eye chakra. Your spirit guides here should also be those of wisdom, grip on reality and a positive mindset in order to not only combat whatever obstacle comes your way but to just stay strong in whatever it is you must deal with for the day, both good and bad.

To focus on the crown chakra, focus on your violets as well as a very bright white and focus on living in the present and moving forward and never looking backward.

While it was said earlier that you're not required to work on all the chakras at the same, your meditation session will actually be more beneficial and even more useful if you do work on all of them in one session. However, if you're a novice meditator when it comes to chakras, just work on one or two at a time until you become advanced enough to where you can start working on all of them in one session. Again, also keep in mind that there is no time limit for these kinds of meditation sessions. It is important to take as much time as you know you truly need. Also, remember to never become angry if your meditation doesn't always turn out to be the way you expect it to. Patience must be learned to have a successful and peaceful meditation session.

Chapter 14

Visualizing your Chakras

Stress is a major culprit in unbalancing and weakening your chakras. It is even worse when you focus only on the stress you're under and you can't relax at all. Another form of meditation in order to keep your chakras aligned and balanced is to picture a certain setting that brings joy and peace to you and imagine yourself in that setting. For example, if you're someone who loves the mountains, picture yourself atop a mountain, surrounded by beautiful trees, clear skies and beautiful water surrounding them. You're in a quiet place yet can hear the pleasant chirping of birds. There is no specific time of day in which to practice this form of meditation, but you should still do this in a quiet, private place free of distractions and seated in a comfortable position on a comfortable piece of furniture, or even the floor with support.

This practice can aid in combatting and not being consumed by stress and its factors.

Chapter 15

Other Remedies for Your Chakras

Some of the following methods on how to repair and keep your chakra points open have been covered in previous chapters, but there are also new methods being introduced here.

Meditation is the most used method of healing and restoring your chakras. It is not limited, however, to your basic practice of sitting in an upright position and crossing your legs. Other meditative activities can include relaxing in or near your garden if you have one. Go for a walk and surround yourself with natural sources such as crystals and grass. Get in touch with your Higher Power. However, whatever it is you choose to do, make sure you refrain from any and all use of electronic objects because part of meditation *is* being in touch with the earth and nature. Also, be sure to make time for breathing exercises in the process.

You must not only visualize your place of joy but also visualize what you would like to see yourself doing about five or ten years from now. While it is important to remain positive during visualization, your dreams and goals still must be realistic, otherwise deluded goals will defeat the purpose of maintaining a healthy third eye chakra.

For crystal healing, place stones around you or on top of you. You could also carry a small bag of gemstones in your bag or pocket wherever you go or wear jewelry made from real gemstones to protect you.

With tense and stiffened muscles and joints, it's near-impossible to keep your chakras in good health, so this is where doing yoga comes into play, not only to help relax the muscles and body, but also the mind.

Acupuncture is also beneficial if you can handle needles because it taps into your pressure points and helps release any and all negative energies from your body.

If you happen to find yourself outgrowing or suddenly becoming disillusioned with your current belief system, and this is not just limited to religion and politics, you know that you have the absolute freedom to change gears to accommodate and enhance YOUR health and well-being, and your ability to transmit warmth and kindness to others.

Drink lots of water, chiefly because it keeps the body healthy by removing and flushing out all the poisons from your body. It also helps keep the mind clear in addition to the body. Water is not limited to ingesting by mouth: everyday practices such as showering/bathing and even washing your dishes by hand produces a calming, cleansing and therapeutic effect.

Don't be afraid to walk outside barefoot. This keeps you in tune and connected with the earth and nature.

Music is also a powerful tool in keeping yourself focused, relaxed, healthy and positive. But remember that there are different types of music for different moods and moments. Use atmospheric, New Age-type music for your meditation sessions or when you're in your bath. Acoustic, indie and jazz music are great for helping enhance and inspire creativity. Try to avoid hard, headbanging music with screaming vocals or any music with negative messages when you're working on keeping your chakras balanced.

You may have never thought about this, but your favorite color may have something to say about your strongest chakra point. For instance, if you tend to gravitate mostly towards the color green, pink or both, your strongest attribute may be the ability to love and your ability and passion to live life to the fullest and find joy even the simplest things in life.

With that being said, a lack or shortage of the color blue in your life might indicate that your throat chakra may not be at its strongest. Select some pieces of clothing that are blue, even if you end up getting yourself just another pair of blue jeans or two.

Fill a room with essential oils such as frankincense (root chakra), juniper (sacral chakra), lemon (navel chakra), rose/rosewood, and basil (heart chakra), lemongrass and blue chamomile (throat chakra), lavender (third eye chakra) and sandalwood (crown chakra). These are best used during yoga and meditation sessions. The proper background music for these sessions is not required, but it does help.

If you feel as if you're doing all that you can to keep your chakras balanced but you aren't achieving the results you want or expect, you may turn to a professional healer or expert for help.

However, you must be sure that the healer knows exactly what he or she is talking about, and isn't using the title of "healer" to appear cool, hip and modern. Spiritual healing is meant to be a way of life, *not* some fleeting, commercialized trend.

Chapter 16

The Five Outer Chakras

Chakra healing and restoration is often focused on the seven main chakras, they often forget that there are actually five more to be implemented along with the seven. The remaining five are all found outside of your body and all have to do with how you connect with the earthly and the spiritual, celestial worlds alike. Another concept to learn from the 12-chakra system is that we as human beings are all connected as one.

Chakra Eight: The Earth Chakra

Located just an inch above the crown chakra, the earth chakra allows you great access to the spiritual worlds and the universe, something that isn't normally humanly possible to achieve. Here, your ego is completely abandoned and you are even more aware of your actions and surroundings. This chakra can even allow you to project your astral form! You cannot fully balance this chakra until you are absolutely certain that your earthly purpose has been fulfilled to its best.

Here, the color to focus on is a deep, ultraviolet light that cannot be seen by humans.

Chakra Nine: The Lunar Chakra

Located about four feet above the crown chakra, this allows you to know firsthand what your true destiny and purpose on this earth are. This chakra consists of three "blueprints":

The healer: Focuses on honing healing skills and learning new ones.

The creator: Focuses on creating new things.

The teacher: Focuses on helping humanity learn.

Note: You cannot be all three at once; you can only be one of the three, depending on your strongest earthly attributes.

Once you do learn the true purpose of your own life, embrace it and don't argue against it, otherwise, this chakra becomes blocked.

Focus on all the colors of the rainbow here because the color really depends on what skill you are learning and accessing.

Chakra Ten: The Solar Chakra

At this stage, you have not only acquired whatever skills you have in the previous stage but now you must utilize them. Located several feet above ground, this enables the ultimate forms of creativity.

Chakra Eleven: The Galactic Chakra

The last three chakras will indeed take rather long to open, depending on energy levels and how fully focused you are, the next and last two will take the longest to achieve because they involve such near-impossible feats as time travel, teleportation, and telekinesis. Once you DO achieve this stage, however, don't forget that these acquired skills are not an excuse to act haughty and that you're higher than any other human. These take discipline and maturity to acquire and maintain. Always take your time when you get to the stage of being able to open this chakra. If you open it too quickly, you will be very damaged and unable to deal with major life changes. This is located 15 feet above the crown chakra and the color of focus is a rose color.

One drawback is that in order to fully activate the skills acquired in this chakra is to open up the 12th chakra.

Chakra Twelve: The Universal Chakra

Your third eye chakra works best in aiding and keeping the universal chakra open and working to its full capacity. In this stage, you have the ability to travel through the universe without limitations.

In order for this chakra to fully function, you must be able to completely detach yourself of any and all forms of materialism. Look at it as though you are actually about to leave this earth for good and you know that your earthly purposes have been fulfilled and you are satisfied. However, be sure that you are completely honest with yourself about this.

Although this chakra is at its highest form of consciousness, it also requires the most healing. Make sure it is reawakened at least every two months. However, once you are fully able to let go of ego and materialism, you have fully matured in terms of consciousness.

Chapter 17

Determining Your Own Chakral Health

Sometimes you will find yourself doubtful if all your chakras are open and healthy. For example, you might notice one day that you have more trouble with open communication with others, something you are normally skillful at. This means you need to work on your throat chakra. However, you can't have a *full* understanding of your chakral health *until* you ask yourself some questions in relation to each of your main chakras. However, in order for these examinations to be fully useful, you need to be completely honest with yourself and have complete, definite answers, with no uncertainties whatsoever. It doesn't matter how negative or positive your answers are, as negative answers will serve as ways of how to improve each chakra. Here is what you need to ask yourself, for each chakra:

Root Chakra

1) Have you received any blessings of late, or at all, in your life?

2) Are any of your beliefs, behaviors, and feelings influenced by family members? Or are they truly *your own* beliefs?

3) What are some traits you have inherited from your parents, both good and bad?

4) What makes you happy, mad or sad?

5) Would you want your family to learn anything from you? If so, what is it?

6) Are you having any kinds of conflicts with people at the moment?

7) Are you superstitious or do you live by certain sentiments, codes, and ideas?

Positive answers to these questions indicate that you are at a steady pace in life and firmly grounded, keeping focused on your tasks and your future, without allowing obstacles to get in your way to stop you. Negative answers will tell you that you need to work on staying focused in order to truly grow as a human being.

Sacral Chakra

The most important aspect of being absolutely sure your emotional health is intact, as well as being sure you don't have any creative blocks on you, is to ask yourself these:

1) What do you do that you consider creative? (It doesn't necessarily *have* to be a fine/visual art, or even music and writing. Some people express their creativity via gardening, landscaping, cooking/baking or even through trades such as welding, roofing, construction and the like) Also, where are you most proficient in your creativity?

2) When you do something creative, in what type of environment would you work best in and feel most alive and/or at peace?

3) What are your dreams in life?

4) Do you indulge in self-criticism, and are you, in turn, easily critical and judgmental of others?

Solar Plexus Chakra

This chakra is the one that takes the most charge of allowing you to develop, determine and maintain your true sense of self. You know you need to work on this chakra if you answer "no" or have otherwise uncertain or outright negative reactions to these questions:

1) Generally speaking, do you like yourself as a person?

2) Are your thoughts, ideas, and mannerisms shaped by yourself *without* the influence of

others? Do you reject the need to be a people pleaser?

3) Can you convey your honest opinions, life, and ideas in a mature, direct and calm manner?

4) Do you consider yourself a mature, responsible person, ready to tackle obstacles and solve problems instead of ignoring or running away from them?

Heart Chakra

In order to fully keep your heart chakra repaired and healthy, make sure you have definite answers, which will either help you continue to strengthen your chakra or work to make improvements and/or any needed changes on it, to these questions:

1) Are you going through any troubling times that interfere with your emotional health? If so, do you know how to let go of all that emotional baggage? And how can you work to fix any problems you currently have, so that you are not, in turn, bitter towards others?

2) Do you have any fears? If so, can you overcome them, and how?

3) Do you have the ability and heart to forgive others for their wrongdoings, especially towards you and/or those you are connected with?

Throat Chakra

Not only does a healthy throat chakra indicate that you are able to express your honest opinions upfront and clearly, but it also means that you know how to express them *constructively* without being harsh, rude or judgmental. And don't appear or be stubborn about your opinions, although you *are* entitled to them. Another important thing to remember is *never* to try and *force* your opinions on others—they have their *own* thoughts, too.

1) How stubborn are you, and how can you correct that?

2) What are your strengths and weaknesses when it comes to honest, effective communication? And what can you do to enhance your communication skills and/or improve them?

Third Eye Chakra

Your third eye chakra is not opened if you find yourself having trouble connecting with your spiritual self. For example, if you are a Christian and find yourself blaming or getting angry with God if something in your life goes wrong or is stressful or even traumatic, then you will have trouble calling onto Him for guidance. While there *are* people in this world who choose not to worship any Deity and instead walk the path of Atheism, having your own spiritual guide is highly beneficial in both times of need and joy. You often hear and notice that a person outright thanks their Deity when something joyful happens in their lives, and ask for help (almost as if as if they're asking a person) in times of trouble and challenge. To make sure *you* not only have a preference of religion or faith but also *keep* your Deity by your side at all times, consider these:

1) What is your spiritual preference? If you *do* have a spiritual preference and a Higher Power to believe in, what do you do to connect with it and *stay* connected? For example, if you are Catholic, do you attend Mass regularly? Do you light candles? Do you partake in reenactments of the Last Supper (Communion)? Do you read your Bible regularly?

2) How connected are you with the spiritual world in general? Do you still find yourself too carnal or

materialistic to *really* keep in touch with your Deity?

Crown Chakra

You know you need to work on strengthening your crown chakra when you feel very disillusioned with life, both carnally *and* spiritually. Another way the crown chakra becomes weakened is if you are so self-absorbed you forget about what's going on in the real world around you and you forget that other people have problems, sometimes even worse and more pressing than yours, too. Even worse is when you forget or even actually aware but refuse to acknowledge that you have problems of your own—that is your inflated ego at work, and at this stage, that kind of ego should have been completely abandoned by now. A person with too much confidence and too-high self-esteem is clearly not connected with their spirituality or the spiritual world. The one thing you can ask yourself is if you have done any form of meditation that day or even recently. If it turns out that you are overdue for a meditation session, you need to get back into the habit of that as soon as possible.

It is very important that you actually take time in scanning your chakra health because if you rush through all these questions just to get through the process, then the process becomes useless, and how can you be completely honest with others in the outside world if you cannot be completely honest with yourself?

Chapter 18

Chakras and Science

Although the concept of chakras has been around for thousands of years and is most closely associated with spirituality, modern science *does* play a part in chakras, especially when it comes to physiology and modern medicine. Every day scientists work to find and sometimes eventually discover treatments and cures for certain diseases, for example by use of certain vaccines. This is also made possible by technological advances, especially those with medical equipment.

All chakra points are placed at certain parts of the body for a reason of balance, as discussed earlier in the book. They are all aligned in the form of a column, like a healthy spine, as the spinal cord is responsible for transmitting messages to your brain as well as maintaining a flow of healthy energy throughout your body. Your nerves and nerve endings are also responsible for these tasks, as the spinal cord cannot do *all* the work. Here are ways that science and the different chakras correlate:

Although the crown chakra and third eye chakras are not located directly at the spinal column, the third eye chakra is connected to the pineal gland, which aids in the release of melatonin which in turn helps to maintain a regular, healthy sleep pattern. It also plays a part in enabling us to have dreams and how they can also help us in the real, waking world.

The crown chakra is connected to the pituitary gland and when the gland is healthy, it keeps hormones under control so that we have the ability to move well, as well as use our sex organs properly to ensure a pleasurable experience.

You don't necessarily need to be "spiritual" to be aware of your surroundings and of others' moods and feelings. It takes a natural capacity of common sense and understanding to do that.

Physical vibrations aren't just some "magic" concepts. Crystals and gemstones *do* play a certain part in producing vibrations, but you also have to move your *own* body. Ever notice any certain vibrations inside of your body when you do yoga, especially if you hold certain poses and stretches for a somewhat prolonged period of time? Those are your nerve endings, muscles and bloodstream at work which also help in clearing your mind. Even a simple standard meditation exercise and the appropriate breathing patterns and depths that go along with it will produce a sudden change of energy in the body, sending messages to your brain that you start to feel more ready to take on whatever life has to throw at you--both good and bad--that day, mind you, all with a clear head and make sure you truly took all the time you needed to complete the meditation exercise for it to fully work for you that day.

Another example of feeling vibration is when you start to feel physically ill, weak or pained when you see or come near a certain person because they create nothing but a cruel, toxic environment for you. This doesn't necessarily mean you are coming down with an illness such as a cold or a virus, it's just your body telling you that you need to get and stay as far away as possible from this person, to prevent yourself from absorbing that person's negative energies which can make you fall ill for real.

Chapter 19

Remember Your Instincts and Your Status as a Human

Although you will have moments where you feel absolutely certain as to which of your chakras needs the most work on a particular day, you will not be one hundred percent sure which of your chakras needs more work than the other and which of them is most important for *you*. It is hard to determine that because all the chakras are supposed to be working together. If one chakra is weakened, yes, it is important that you work on that one, but it is more than likely at least one other chakra will need to be worked on afterward. In order to maintain chakral health, you must make sure you eat healthily and avoid foods that aren't healthy or that your body cannot tolerate, exercise as regularly as your able-bodiedness allows.

More importantly, if you KNOW of a certain place or person that makes you feel negative emotions or vibrations inside your body, stay away and avoid it as much as possible. For example, if there is a rough section of town where physical fights (especially when weapons are involved) and drug activity occur on a regular basis, especially during the evening/night, avoid that area like the plague, because if you don't, then you are only playing with fire. So, if you find yourself passing this dangerous part of town on your commute home from work or wherever, plan a different route home, even if it takes longer than your current route. Changing your route will prevent you from becoming a "bundle of nerves", which will cause you to lose concentration on your driving and worse, cause you to be in a car accident.

Tapering off that scenario, there are people, especially those who belong to the Catholic faith, who keep pieces of symbolism such as the rosary, a figurine of the Virgin Mary or any items related to Saint Christopher, the patron saint of safe traveling mercies in their vehicles for protection. Those from other faiths may even also keep gemstones or beads hanging from their rearview mirrors. These will help in keeping them safe, less anxious and focused on the roads, but they will not make the dangerous areas any safer to be in, and these items are also not intended to be used as substitutes for using caution and common sense while driving. This also means that if you see construction being done on a highway and a sign directs you to a detour, *take that detour!*

If you constantly feel sluggish, pained, worried or ill at your current job because of the toxic environment* created by rude and/or lazy coworkers and managers, start looking for another job as quickly as possible and dedicate yourself to applying for a new job. At the same time, it is wise to just stay at your current job for financial security until you do finally land yourself a new one. In the meantime, *completely* ignore anything rude or asinine your managers or coworkers say to you because the more reactionary you are to them, the more depressed and upset you come, and this leads to poor job performance on *your* part. With that being said, don't use the fact that you're looking for a new job as an excuse to perform your tasks hastily and poorly, or slack off and shirk your responsibilities altogether. Also definitely don't start to act as mean as the rest of the staff does just so that you don't feel left out or insecure. If you adopt and mimic their lazy and rude attitudes, then you're only stooping down to their toxic levels, and you'll even end up pushing away those who actually are good to you and truly care that you succeed not only professionally but personally as well.

*I actually keep an amethyst stone and a hematite stone at my desk at work because I myself work in a negative environment at times. The amethyst is to keep my head clear and to keep me from losing focus on my tasks (I work in dealing with medical records, which requires *very serious and strong* attention to detail to avoid HIPAA Law violations) and I use the hematite to prevent me from allowing the negative attitudes of others from getting to me so that I don't end up too physically or emotionally pained to perform my tasks properly—or even at all. I don't use these stones to force someone else to be positive, mind you, nor do I use them to make myself oblivious and uncaring, but to not allow someone else's baggage to become my own. Another way I have somehow survived so much negativity at my workplace enough to leave for the day feeling better is by keeping healthy eating habits and avoiding junky fast food, while at the same time treating myself to pastries every now and then.

On a more positive note, say if you work in a field that requires you to give public speaking presentations on a regular basis. One morning a normally confident and upfront you may wake up feeling nervous and anxious, worried you might forget what you will have to say as part of your presentation and fear your colleagues will laugh at or ridicule you, then you need to keep your throat chakra open for that event. Here are some tips for that:

1) Wear something blue that day, such as a sweater or suit (depending on your company's dress code requirements). Even simple blue pieces of jewelry would suffice.

2) If you have time to eat breakfast at home, you can incorporate something like blueberries into your oatmeal or whatever quick breakfast item you prefer to partake in. You could also fix yourself some lemongrass tea. A bonus is if you have a blue thermos to just take your tea on-the-go with you.

3) Carry crystals, particularly those in the blue color family, in your pocket or bag with you.

Chapter 20

The Importance of a Support System

While it *is* important to have private time for yourself during meditation and other practices, it is also important to have a set of friends who truly encourage and care for your health and well-being, on both spiritual and worldly levels. Here are some ways that you and your friends can help uplift and encourage each other:

1) Attend a mass meditation event or a yoga class together. However, keep in mind if you and/or your friends feel any vibes that the attendees are just there to look hip and cool and to act holier-than-thou, immediately leave those places and form your own yoga and meditation sessions elsewhere.

2) If you have a shared love for gardening, plant a garden together.

3) Have a meal together out at a healthy restaurant or even cook a healthy meal together at home.

4) Go hiking, kayaking or do something nature-based together.

5) Visit an art museum or attend a music concert to encourage each other's creative juices.

Chapter 21

How Reiki Helps Rebalance Your Chakras

Due to life's everyday stresses, such as work, bills, managing finances and others, it's only natural that your chakras will most likely become misaligned. That stress in turn will pain your body *physically,* because the energy cannot flow through your body. Reiki will work well in helping ease and/or alleviating this pain because the Reiki practitioner knows *exactly* where your chakra points are. Here is what the practitioner will focus on, as far as ailments go, in relation to each chakra:

Root Chakra

When this chakra is imbalanced, you will experience ailments such as lower back pain, sciatica as well as problems with the groin, hips, knees, ankles, feet and calves. Once Reiki is performed on these areas, you will feel more grounded and less likely to, or even longer, experience these pains.

Sacral Chakra

Any form of sexual tension, abuse or just a lack of libido will block this chakra. A blocked sacral also stems from reproductive system-related ailment such as cystic fibrosis, as well as pelvic and lower back pains. Reiki healing can help you outwardly express your current emotions, including any issues you may have with your romantic relationship and any sexual frustration, so that you can completely heal. It will also help lift the creative block you might have in you.

Navel Chakra

This chakra is blocked especially when your self-esteem is low, and because of that you might have liver and stomach issues or feel very weak and depressed. Reiki helps with restoring your self-esteem in order to focus on your daily tasks and looking forward to what the future will hold for you.

Heart Chakra

An imbalanced heart chakra may lead to respiratory and pulmonary issues and in some cases even worse: heart disease or heart failure, or even breast or lung cancer. Many of the negative feelings and thoughts associated with this imbalance are depression, inability to give love and compassion, feelings of loneliness. In order to be able to love again and in return receive love and compassion from others, many will turn to Reiki healing for help.

Throat Chakra

As a blocked throat chakra is associated with an inability to express your true feelings and thoughts, preferably in a constructive manner, these are the ailments that might come along with this blockage: thyroid problems, swollen glands and a sore throat. Reiki healing helps with this in

order for us to be able to express our true selves
and achieve our true goals, without the fear of
being ridiculed or judged.

Third Eye Chakra

A stroke, brain tumor (or even a hemorrhage) and
neurological issues may result from a blocked
third eye chakra, especially when your perception
of reality and depth are both off and when you do
not trust your instincts and intuition. Reiki will
help you learn to not have these kinds of trust
issues so that you have a better grip on reality and
see beyond things in the world that many are
shortsighted and unaware about.

Crown Chakra

The most prominent ailments that come along
with having a blocked crown chakra are chronic
fatigue (unrelated to pain or illness) and
depression. It also causes you lose touch not only
with your higher power, but also the Universe,
thus making you shortsighted and bitter towards

everyone for no reason. Reiki will help you get back in touch with your higher power and help you realize and see the good things the Universe has to offer you.

Conclusion

Please keep in mind that the concepts in this book are *not* to be dismissed as a form of modern pseudo-spirituality nor are they to be used as ways to block out reality or shirk your life responsibilities. Nor should you act as if you are better than anyone else. Instead, use this book as a guide to help you deal with rougher times and obstacles in a positive, healthy way. Remember, a positive energy and attitude always win!

Love and Best Wishes

Thank you!

Before you go, I just wanted to say thank you for purchasing my book.

You could have picked from dozens of other books on the same topic but you took a chance and chose this one.

So, a HUGE thanks to you for getting this book and for reading all the way to the end.

Now I wanted to ask you for a small favor. Could you please take just a few minutes to leave a review for this book on Amazon?

This feedback will help me continue to write the type of books that will help you get the results you want. So if you enjoyed it, please let me know! (-: